The Prism of Leadership

OrangeBooks Publication

1st Floor, Rajhans Arcade, Mall Road, Kohka, Bhilai, Chhattisgarh 490020
Website: **www.orangebooks.in**

First Edition, 2026

ISBN: 978-93-7426-475-1

Price: Rs. 299.00

Printed in India

THE PRISM OF LEADERSHIP

LEADERSHIP BEYOND TITLES

VISHAL SONAWANE

OrangeBooks Publication
www.orangebooks.in

Testimonial for "The Prism of Leadership"

Big words, borrowed models, and memorable slogans are frequently used when discussing leadership. The Leadership Prism is distinct. It does not attempt to win the reader over. It makes an effort to clarify things. And that's its greatest strength, in my opinion.

Vishal views leadership as a perspective rather than a title or level of authority. Here, the concept of a "prism" function flawlessly. Leadership is not a single, set trait or approach. Situations, people, pressure, and responsibility all affect it.

This book acknowledges that leadership is dynamic rather than static. It stays clear of the trap of providing a single, all-encompassing formula.

The book strikes a good balance between doing and thinking from a management perspective. It makes the connection between inner clarity and external behaviour, which is something that many leadership books discuss but seldom adequately explain. It feels very real to emphasise self-awareness, ownership, and making decisions in ambiguous circumstances. In Indian organisations, where hierarchy, emotions, and execution all work together, these are common problems. The grounded tone is what I found appealing. The concepts are useful without being overly simplistic. The insights carry authority, yet leave space for the reader's own judgment. Because of this, the book applies to both young managers and seasoned leaders who are prepared to take a break, think things through, and develop.

- Dr Abhijeett Desai

Innovation Consultant | Author | Leadership Coach

Dedication

To every leader who believes leadership is not a title but a responsibility to inspire and transform.

Author's Note

Vishal Sonawane is an accomplished Entrepreneurship and Business Coach with over 16 years of expertise in Learning and Development. He has partnered with organisations across diverse industries to design leadership strategies, build future-ready leaders, and foster cultures of innovation and growth. Known for his practical frameworks and transformative approach, Vishal empowers businesses to align leadership development with strategic goals, ensuring measurable impact and sustainable success.

Acknowledgments

I want to express my heartfelt gratitude to everyone who contributed to this journey.

To my family, for their unwavering support and encouragement. To my mentors and colleagues in the Learning & Development space, who inspired me to think differently and innovate. To the organisations and leaders I've worked with over the past 16 years, your challenges and aspirations shaped the ideas in this book. And to every reader who picks up this book, you are the reason this work exists. Thank you for believing in leadership that transforms people and organisations.

Feed Forward

Why this book Matters

'Leadership' is a big word in today's corporate, bureaucratic, and organisational world. Everyone talks about taking the lead. Most of the time, these conversations revolve around being proactive, taking initiative, or being the front face of a task. Some organisations expect you to lead, while others hesitate to give you that responsibility because of your designation.

Across organisations, departments, teams, and individuals, the scenario is the same

- All of us want to be leaders.
- Most of us want to take the lead.
- Some want to contribute to leadership without criticising.
- None of us wants to fail as a leader.

But here's the truth — **leadership doesn't happen overnight**.

So, how do we become leaders who know how to be proactive, take initiative, walk the talk, communicate effectively, and demonstrate all the qualities that define true leadership?

This book introduces **The Prism of Leadership**—a framework that I have developed after years of observing and understanding practical challenges faced by organisations and individuals. Most existing tools are either outdated or too complex for today's dynamic business environment. While challenges may seem similar to the past, they require a **modern, focused approach**. I wanted to create a tool that is **easy to use, practical, and implementable**—a tool that organisations and individuals can adopt without confusion.

This implementable tool will also be available through our **Leadership Assessment Centre**, ensuring that development is not just theoretical but measurable and actionable.

Organisational culture, performance, and values are reflected through employees. These employees operate within a hierarchy, and leadership begins when people start driving the organisation's vision.

Every organisation has a hierarchy, and each level of that hierarchy requires not only personal leadership but also the right **Knowledge, Skills, and Attitude** to perform effectively and help others succeed. This book will show you how to develop these qualities systematically, using a practical framework that empowers leaders and builds future-ready organisations.

This book is designed for **Junior management, Mid and Senior Management levels and Executive level of organisations like CEOs, business owners, trainers, and as a reference for MBA/PGDBA students**—anyone who aspires to lead effectively and create impact. Whether you are managing a team, driving organisational strategy, or preparing for leadership roles, this book will help you:

- **Understand leadership beyond titles** and develop the mindset to lead with clarity.
- **Adopt a practical framework** (The Prism of Leadership) to measure and improve leadership competencies.
- **Empower teams and build a leadership culture** that drives organisational growth.
- **Use actionable tools and templates** for assessment, development, and benchmarking.
- **Create future-ready leaders** through structured succession planning and measurable progress.

"At the end of this book, you'll find a comprehensive toolkit in the Appendix — ready-to-use templates, universal question sets, and interpretation guides to make implementation seamless."

"Now that you know why leadership transformation matters, let's explore why titles don't make leaders—and what truly does."

Index

Chapter - 1
Leadership Beyond Titles 1

Chapter - 2
The Prism Concept.. 9

Chapter - 3
Seven Colours of Leadership 18

Chapter - 4
The Refraction Strategy 30

Chapter - 5
The Prism Matrix 44

Chapter - 6
Organisational Application 61

Chapter - 7
Driving Organisational Impact Through Results ... 71

Chapter - 8
Case Studies & Scenarios 77

Chapter - 9
Conclusion – Becoming the Change Catalyst........ 91

Appendix **95**

Chapter - 1
Leadership Beyond Titles

Section A: What Leadership Really Means

- Quotes from Warren Bennis & Dr. A.P.J. Abdul Kalam.
- Leadership as attitude, not title.

"Leadership is the capacity to translate vision into reality."

– Warren Bennis.

Doesn't this statement give a clear picture of a Visionary leader who has the power and authority to bring the vision into reality? It is indeed a strong image of a leader. We all believe and want it to happen.

I have seen such visionary leaders. However, not all leaders are visionary, and not all those who can bring others' visions to reality are visionary. This also works because we need leaders who can work together, and that requires a different competency. At some point, a leader seeking growth in terms of designation, authority, responsibilities, and credibility needs to develop these competencies.

Let us look at the second thought from the well-known and loved personality from India.

"A leader must have vision and passion and not be afraid of any problem. Instead, he should know how to defeat it."

–Dr A.P.J. Abdul Kalam.

What we see here is again a great visionary leader, passionate, a problem solver and the one who can come over from any situation. Isn't it thought-provoking too?

Leadership sounds inspiring and interesting when defined by great thinkers. But what does it look like in practice? In many Indian or foreign organisations, leadership is often misunderstood. Promotions are based on seniority or past performance, not on leadership capability. A good engineer becomes a plant head. A top salesperson becomes a sales manager. But leadership is not about doing your old job well—it's about enabling others to do theirs better. Your field of expertise may remain the same.

Our teacher never selected me as a monitor for the class, and that upset me many times. The teacher often scolded the monitors by saying, "You are the monitor, and you should be more responsible." I never thought of becoming a monitor. Now my daughter comes and tells me how she has become a monitor, and from her 1st standard to date, she has been a monitor every year. She loves to share her school stories of how she maintained discipline in class.

Once, I casually asked her, “Don’t you do masti (Naughtiness) in class?” As expected, she replied, “If I do that, then how can I be a monitor or lead them?” I realised why I never became a class monitor.

Leadership is not about making others work; it is working with them and inspiring them to.

This raises a question of how many organisations take the internal mobility concept or the Development Function of HR seriously.

Because if we go by these definitions of internal mobility or development functions, they are absolutely correct. However, except for a few organisations, these functions rarely address how an individual can become a leader or what it truly takes to transform oneself as a leader.

When we go out on our consultation visits or L&D projects, we often hear that they could have promoted me, but instead hired someone from outside, which is a common piece of feedback. Sometimes, it is clearly visible to us that an employee with good knowledge and skills is not promoted or given a designation deserved because of **Their Attitude or approach.** Believe me, there could be a lot of such scenarios. Not judging anyone because of it. Organisations need to be practical and thorough. They must choose the right approach to transform the employees they have with them, where they have already invested.

Section B: The Reality of Leadership Today

- Expanded explanations of seniority bias, performance trap, comfort zone leadership.

The Reality of Leadership Today

Seniority Bias

In many organisations, loyalty is often rewarded with promotions. Someone who has been with the company for 15 or 20 years is seen as "deserving" of a leadership role. But tenure alone doesn't guarantee leadership capability. It creates a situation where experience is valued over adaptability, and the organisation risks stagnation.

Performance Trap

High performers in technical roles often get promoted to managerial positions. A great engineer becomes a plant head, or a top salesperson becomes a sales manager. But leadership is not about doing your old job well—it's about enabling others to do theirs better. Without training, these promotions can lead to frustration for both the leader and the team.

Comfort Zone Leadership

Many leaders cling to old methods because "this is how we've always done it." They resist change, avoid innovation, and prefer the safety of familiar processes. This mindset hinders progress and renders organisations vulnerable in a rapidly changing business environment.

Title vs. Transformation

A designation gives authority, but not influence. True leadership is about transformation—of people, processes, and culture. Without this, a leader is just a manager with a title, not a catalyst for growth.

We learn from others. So, let me narrate a story, and we will go through this story to understand our implementable leadership technique.

Section C: VMPL Story – Setting the Context for our Journey

- VMPL's growth, challenges, and leadership gaps.

VMPL's Story: Versatile Manufacturing Pvt. Ltd.

In 1987, Mr Sudhakar Patil started **Versatile Manufacturing Pvt. Ltd. (VMPL)** in a small industrial shed in Pune. The company began by making rubber bushes and washers—simple components, but with precision and reliability. Over the years, VMPL grew steadily. By the late 90s, they were manufacturing clutch plates for major automotive brands. Today, VMPL is a ₹250 crore company with 800 employees and a reputation for quality.

But growth brings its own challenges. VMPL still runs on traditional processes—paper trails, manual approvals, and a comfort zone that employees are reluctant to leave. Attrition has climbed to **31%**, and leadership decisions often follow a familiar pattern:

- "He's been with us for 15 years, promote him."
- "She's our best performer, make her the manager."

When Ananya joined as Chief Customer Care Manager, she saw the cracks immediately. Her team hadn't received training for three years. Complaints piled up:

- Phones unanswered by sales staff.
- No visits to smaller accounts.
- Warranty issues unresolved.
- Engineers disorganised, requiring multiple visits.

The team was experienced but stagnant. They knew their jobs but lacked the mindset to improve. Ananya realised that VMPL didn't just need process changes—it needed a **leadership transformation.**

This is not unique to VMPL. Many organisations promote people based on **seniority or past performance**, not leadership capability. A good engineer becomes a plant head. A top salesperson becomes a sales manager. But leadership is not about doing your old job well—it's about enabling others to do theirs better.

Section D: Introducing the Prism Concept

- Why leadership needs transformation.
- Reflection questions.

The Leader as a Prism

A prism doesn't just exist—it transforms. Similarly, a leader is not just a title; a leader is the prism that refracts raw potential in their team into a vibrant spectrum of competencies.

- A true leader develops people.
- They instil key skills like communication, decision-making, and adaptability.
- They create an environment where individuals grow beyond their current capabilities.

At VMPL, this was missing. Leaders were not acting as prisms—they were acting as filters, limiting growth instead of enabling it.

Why Leadership Development Matters?

Ignoring leadership capability comes at a cost

- High attrition (VMPL's 31% is a warning sign).
- Stagnation in processes and innovation.
- Missed opportunities for growth and competitiveness.

Leadership development is not optional—it's the foundation for organisational success. When leaders act as prisms, they don't just achieve targets—they transform people, teams, and the organisation.

The Insight

Leadership is not a reward for tenure or performance. It's an attitude, a behaviour, a commitment to growth. Titles don't create leaders—refraction does. Just as a prism transforms plain white light into a vibrant spectrum, true leadership transforms raw potential into a range of competencies.

Reflection Questions

- In your organisation, how are leaders chosen—by tenure, performance, or leadership capability?
- What risks do you see in promoting without assessing leadership readiness?
- If you were Ananya, where would you start?

"We've seen the reality of leadership today. But how do we transform it? Enter the Prism Concept—a simple yet powerful framework."

Chapter - 2
The Prism Concept

Section A

- Why are we talking Prism?
- Metaphor explained
- Leader as a prism for others

Section A: Why are we talking Prism?

Some time ago, our team conducted a sales training program for the Regional Sales Managers of a leading automotive manufacturer. During the session, every participant insisted on keeping their mobile phones. When asked why, they said, *"Our mobile phone is our life. If we are not available, our team cannot make decisions. We guide them, handle escalations, and manage sales. We are the most important people in the organisation."*

We asked them a simple question

"If you leave this organisation tomorrow, will the business shut down completely? Or will there just be a small dip?"

The silence in the room said it all.

These managers believed that constant calls and being available 24/7 made them indispensable. In reality, it revealed something else—they had not empowered their teams to make decisions independently. They liked the dependency. They were managing, not leading. True leadership is not about being the busiest person in the room; it's about building a team that thrives without you.

Why do some leaders shine while others remain ordinary, even when they have similar experience and qualifications?

The answer lies in the transformation—just like a prism turns plain white light into a vibrant spectrum. Leadership works the same way. Without transformation, potential remains plain and unremarkable.

VMPL's Reality

When Ananya joined VMPL as Chief Customer Care Manager, she quickly realised that the company's leadership structure was built on a familiar formula:

- Promote those who have been around the longest.
- Reward top performers with managerial titles.

On paper, this looked fair. In practice, it created a leadership team that was strong in technical knowledge but weak in adaptability, communication, and people development. They were excellent at managing tasks but struggled to inspire, coach, and transform their teams. Ananya also tried to tell them that she may not be the right person to handle the quality. Some of the team members were unhappy with this management decision, too.

"They know," Ananya thought, "but they aren't refracting it into leadership."

The Leader as a Prism

A prism doesn't just exist—it transforms. Similarly, a leader does not merely hold a title; **a leader is the prism** that refracts the raw potential of their team into a vibrant spectrum of competencies.

- A true leader develops people.
- They instil key skills like communication, decision-making, and adaptability.
- They create an environment where individuals grow beyond their current capabilities.

Section B: VMPL Story – Resistance and Awareness

- Leaders are realising gaps.

At VMPL, this was missing. Leaders were acting as filters—passing light through without change—instead of prisms that bend, adapt, and create transformation.

What Does the Prism Represent?

Think of leadership as a prism

- **White Light:** Raw potential—skills, experience, certifications.
- **Prism Faces:** Knowledge, Skills, Attitude.

- **Spectrum:** Seven leadership competencies (VIBGYOR).

Every leader begins as **white light**—a source of raw potential made up of skills, experience, and qualifications. But potential alone doesn't create impact. It needs direction, focus, and transformation.

That's where the **prism of leadership** comes in. This prism has three critical faces: **Knowledge, Skills, and Attitude (KSA)**. When potential passes through these faces, it refracts into a vibrant **spectrum of seven leadership competencies—our VIBGYOR**.

This transformation is what separates good managers from great leaders. Without the prism, potential remains plain. With it, leaders shine across every dimension—driving results, inspiring teams, and shaping the future.

Section C: Faces of the Prism

- Knowledge, Skills, Attitude.

The Three Faces of the Prism

Every prism has faces. In leadership, these faces are

- **Knowledge:** Industry expertise, product understanding, process know-how

  VMPL managers had plenty of this—they knew clutch plates inside out.

- **Skills:** Communication, decision-making, execution.

  This was missing—customer complaints piled up because managers couldn't coordinate effectively.

- **Attitude:** Openness, adaptability, ethical behaviour.

  Comfort zones ruled at VMPL— "This is how we've always done it" was the mantra.

Without these three faces working together, the prism cannot refract light. Similarly, without knowledge, skills, and attitude aligned, leadership cannot create impact.

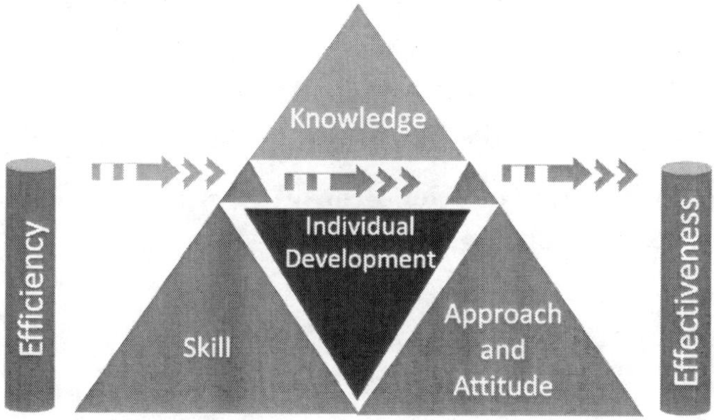

Leadership complexity varies, and prism types help visualise this

- **Triangular Prism:** Focused leadership for small teams.
- **Rectangular Prism:** Structured leadership for mid-sized organisations.
- **Polygonal Prism:** Complex leadership for global enterprises.

Quick Prism Type Selector – 3 Questions

1. **How many departments or functions do you manage?**
   - 1–2 → Triangular
   - 3–5 → Rectangular
   - 6+ → Polygonal
2. **Do you work with multiple geographies or external partners?**
   - Yes → Polygonal
   - No → Triangular or Rectangular
3. **How often do you deal with cross-functional decision-making?**
   - Rarely → Triangular
   - Frequently → Rectangular
   - Daily → Polygonal

VMPL Example

VMPL started with a triangular prism approach—simple and focused. As it grew to ₹250 crore turnover and added multiple functions, it needed a rectangular prism mindset. Today, with global suppliers and innovation demands, VMPL is moving toward a polygonal prism approach.

In this book, we will primarily use the **Triangular Prism** for practical implementation because it offers clarity and simplicity for most organisations.

However, leadership complexity varies, and advanced prism types—Rectangular and Polygonal—can provide deeper insights for organisations managing multi-functional or global challenges

(If you want to explore these advanced applications and digital tools, connect with us through our Leadership Assessment Centre).

Why Refraction Matters

Refraction is a change. It's bending old habits, challenging comfort zones, and adapting to new realities. For VMPL, refraction meant:

- Moving from paper trails to digital processes.
- Training managers in people skills, not just technical know-how.
- Building a culture of accountability and innovation.

Without refraction, VMPL faced

- High attrition (31%).
- Stagnation in innovation.
- Missed growth opportunities.

Section D: Transition to VIBGYOR

- How competencies emerge as colours.

➢ **Transition to VIBGYOR**

When white light passes through a prism, it becomes a spectrum of seven colours. In leadership, these colours represent seven competencies:

➢ **Violet – Vision & Strategic Thinking.**

Violet is associated with wisdom, imagination, and foresight—perfect for vision and strategy.

- **Indigo – Integrity & Ethics**

Indigo represents depth and truth, aligning with ethical leadership and strong values

- **Blue – Communication & Influence**

Blue symbolises clarity and trust, essential for effective communication and influence.

- **Green – Growth & Innovation**

Green is linked to growth, creativity, and renewal—ideal for innovation and continuous improvement

- **Yellow – Decision-Making & Problem Solving**

Yellow signifies optimism and clarity, which are critical for confident decision-making.

- **Orange – People Management & Coaching**

Orange reflects warmth and energy, representing people-centric leadership and empowerment.

- **Red – Execution & Results Orientation**

Red stands for action, urgency, and results—perfect for execution and accountability.

In the next chapter, we'll explore each colour in detail and see how VMPL can use this framework to transform its leadership culture.

Reflection Questions

- Which face of the prism—Knowledge, Skills, or Attitude—do you think is strongest in your leadership style?
- Where do you need refraction? Where are you still "white light"?
- How will you start aligning KSAs in your team?

"The Prism refracts potential into colours. Next, let's decode these seven colours and what they mean for leadership."

Chapter - 3
Seven Colours of Leadership

Section A: Why Colours Matter

- Leadership is not black and white

The way we look through our eyes, the world is never black and white. We see colours everywhere—each with its own meaning. So why do we often view employees in black and white—good or bad, performer or non-performer? Leadership is not monochrome. Every colour in the Prism of Leadership has significance. Each colour represents a competency that transforms people—and when people grow, organisations thrive.

The Prism of Leadership is not only about how you change people but also how each colour brings organisational growth. By now, you must have understood that we are not only talking about the organisation—we are talking about transforming people.

Why Colours Matter

Colours in the Prism Framework represent **seven leadership competencies** that every leader needs to develop in themselves and their teams. These competencies are not isolated — they work together to create empowered individuals who drive organisational success. When leaders embrace these colours, they stop being bottlenecks and start being catalysts for growth.

Section B: VIBGYOR Framework

- **Each colour explained with:**
    - Significance (blended reasoning).
    - VMPL example.
    - Expected actions.

The Seven Colours of Leadership

Violet – Vision & Strategic Thinking

- **Significance:** Vision and strategic thinking are critical traits because if you do not think of the future as a leader, you will lead for now—but not forever. Leaders must anticipate change and prepare their teams for transformation.
- **VMPL Example:** Managers focused only on production targets, ignoring digital transformation and market trends.
- **FMCG Industry Example (Consulting Experience):** An FMCG client halted a transformation project because the HR Head felt uncomfortable when we challenged existing formats. The resistance showed a lack of strategic foresight and fear of necessary change.

  This incident reflected a larger issue: **when leaders resist questions, they limit strategic thinking and block organisational growth.**

- **Expected Action:** Conduct quarterly strategy sessions with teams. Share organisational goals and explain how each department contributes to the bigger picture.

Indigo – Integrity & Ethics

- **Significance:** Integrity or ethics is not a board we hang on our neck—it's a cultural practice. Every step an organisation takes must be rooted in ethics and monitored consistently. This colour ensures trust and credibility at every level.
- **VMPL Example:** Warranty complaints revealed gaps in ethical handling of customer issues, damaging trust.
- **FMCG Industry Example:** In one FMCG company, integrity was a stated core value, yet leaders believed they could speak to employees in any manner as long as results improved. KPI changes were needed, but the deeper issue was respecting employees' emotions and maintaining dignity—core elements of integrity.
- **Expected Action:** Build compliance into daily processes. Leaders must lead by example—no shortcuts, no compromises.

Blue – Communication & Influence

- **Significance:** Communication and influence ease or save lots of time. They pave the road for solution-building and prevent confusion. Clear communication accelerates decision-making and builds trust.

- **VMPL Example:** Customer care calls were transferred without solutions—a sign of poor communication and lack of ownership.
- **Retail industry (Consulting experience):** A retail operations team kept missing deadlines because leaders communicated tasks verbally without written clarity. Confusion spreads simply due to unclear messaging.
- **Expected Action:** Hold weekly team huddles. Train managers in active listening and clear messaging. Encourage open dialogue.

Green – Growth & Innovation

- **Significance:** We all want to grow and innovate, but the actual meaning of these terms is often misunderstood. Growth and innovation require creativity—and they can start at any level of the organisation. Leaders must create space for ideas and experimentation.
- **VMPL Example:** Resistance to digitalisation showed a lack of an innovative mindset, slowing progress.
- **Manufacturing Training Experience:** One of our long-term manufacturing clients, with whom we've partnered for over six years, consistently resisted revising training content or adopting new methods. While other clients welcomed fresh approaches, this organisation preferred repeating the same modules, which limited innovation and slowed skill enhancement.

- **Expected Action:** Launch small innovation projects. Reward creative ideas. Encourage teams to challenge "the way we've always done it."

Yellow – Decision-Making & Problem Solving

- **Significance:** Most complex and simple problems can be solved—but as a leader, you are forming this habit and mindset in your people. Decision-making is not just about speed; it's about building confidence and agility across the organisation.
- **VMPL Example:** Engineers needed multiple visits because decisions were delayed, frustrating customers.
- **Onsite Consulting Experience:** During a process audit, we recommended a few operational changes. The GM–Operations immediately said he couldn't decide and that only the CEO could take the call. This overdependence on a single decision-maker slowed execution and reduced accountability.
- **Expected Action:** Use data-driven decision frameworks. Empower team leads to make decisions within defined boundaries.

Orange – People Management & Coaching

- **Significance:** Leaders act as teachers, coaches, mentors, and trainers. Empowerment and equipping people to the right extent are the needs of the hour. This colour reduces dependency and builds future leaders.

- **VMPL Example:** Managers liked being the “go-to” person, creating dependency and limiting team growth.
- **HR Leadership Example:** In a discussion with an HR Head, he proudly mentioned that his assistant wasn’t formally trained in HR but simply executed whatever instructions he gave. This reflected a task-based approach rather than true people development or coaching.
- **Expected Action:** Delegate responsibilities. Create mentoring plans. Focus on developing team autonomy.

Red – Execution & Results Orientation

- **Significance:** All plans fail without execution. Ownership, responsibility, and accountability help leaders deliver results and sustain performance. Execution converts vision into reality.
- **VMPL Example:** Focus on quantity over quality led to customer dissatisfaction and repeated complaints.
- **Real-life Sales Execution case:** I once worked with a Sales GM who broke almost every colour in the VIBGYOR spectrum—especially Red. His entire focus was on hitting numbers, and while he consistently achieved targets, his approach relied purely on aggression. There was no emphasis on process, discipline, or sustainable execution. As a result, his team struggled to match his intensity, and his performance became inconsistent.

- **Expected Action:** Set clear KPIs. Monitor progress regularly. Celebrate achievements and address gaps promptly.

Section C: Priority Coding

- Immediate, Enhance, Monitor.
- Summary table.

How Colours Drive Empowerment

When leaders develop these competencies, they empower their teams to take ownership. Dependency reduces, decision-making improves, and innovation thrives. This is how leadership transforms people—and transformed people transform organisations.

Prism Matrix Preview

We can use 'The Prism Matrix' as a simple yet powerful tool to measure leadership transformation. It helps leaders assess their own competencies and track how they empower their teams.

We will discuss in Chapter 4, i.e. refraction strategy, how we arrived at this scoring or scoreboard in detail. This section is to provide an overview or representation of how this will look.

Below is an example for VMPL

- **0** = No capability demonstrated
- **1** = Very low capability
- **2** = Basic capability
- **3** = Moderate capability
- **4** = Strong capability
- **5** = Excellent / Role model capability

Color	Competency	Leader Current Score	Leader Target Score	Team Current Score	Team Target Score
Violet	Vision & Strategic Thinking	2	4	1	3
Indigo	Integrity & Ethics	3	5	2	4
Blue	Communication & Influence	2	4	2	4
Green	Growth & Innovation	1	3	1	3
Yellow	Decision-Making & Problem Solving	1	4	2	4
Orange	People Management & Coaching	1	4	1	3
Red	Execution & Results Orientation	1	5	2	4

How to Interpret This Matrix

- **Leader Columns:** Show where the leader stands today and where they need to be.
- **Team Columns:** Reflect the team's current capability and target for empowerment.

- This reinforces the concept that **leaders first transform themselves (white light → spectrum)** and then **act as prisms to refract their team's potential into colours**.

The next thing we will look at is the priority coding. The priority coding tells us about the intensity of actions to be taken by the leaders.

Priority Coding Summary Table Example

Gap Calculation

Gap = Target Score – Current Score

(Target is usually 4 or 5 for leadership competencies).

Priority Levels

- Gap ≥ 3 → Immediate Attention

  Example: Current score = 1, Target = 4 → Gap=3

  → This competency needs urgent development.

- Gap = 1–2 → Enhance

  Example: Current score = 2, Target = 4 → Gap=2

  → Needs improvement but not critical.

- Gap = 0 → Monitor

  Example: Current score = 4, Target = 4 → Gap=0

  → Maintain and reinforce.

Immediate Attention ***Enhance*** ***Monitor***

Now, if we take the example of the above table, priority coding will look like this. Priority Coding helps us in deciding the action urgency.

- **Violet:** Leader 2→4 → Gap = 2 → Enhance; Team 1→3→ Gap = 2 → Enhance
- **Indigo:** Leader 3→5 → Gap = 2 → Enhance; Team 2→4 → Gap = 2 → Enhance
- **Blue:** Leader 2→4 → Gap = 2 → Enhance; Team 2→4→ Gap = 2 → Enhance
- **Green:** Leader 1→3 → Gap = 2 → Enhance; Team 1→3 → Gap = 2 → Enhance
- **Yellow:** Leader 1→4 → Gap = 3 → Immediate; Team 2→4 → Gap = 2 → Enhance
- **Orange:** Leader 1→4 → Gap = 3 → Immediate; Team 1→3 → Gap = 2 → Enhance
- **Red:** Leader 1→5 → Gap = 3 → Immediate; Team 2→4→ Gap = 2 → Enhance

Color	Competency	Leader priority	Team priority
Violet	Vision & Strategic Thinking	Enhance	Enhance
Indigo	Integrity & Ethics	Enhance	Enhance
Blue	Communication & Influence	Enhance	Enhance
Green	Growth & Innovation	Enhance	Enhance
Yellow	Decision-Making & Problem Solving	Immediate	Enhance
Orange	People Management & Coaching	Immediate	Enhance
Red	Execution & Results Orientation	Immediate	Enhance

This table gives leaders a clear roadmap

- **Immediate Attention:** Red, Orange, Yellow
- **Enhance:** Green, Blue, Indigo, Violet
- **Monitor:** Currently, it is blank, and not necessary that it will be blank. When one or two colours change under the refraction index, they will fall under the monitor.

Reflection Questions

- Which colour do you think is missing in your leadership style?
- Which colour is most critical for your organisation right now?
- How will you start building these colours in your team?

"Knowing the colours is not enough. How do we create transformation? That's where the Refraction Strategy comes in."

Chapter - 4
The Refraction Strategy

Section A: Dual Transformation

- Leader transforms self, then team.

Dual Transformation Role

Leadership transformation happens in two stages

1. **Stage One: Transform Yourself**

Every leader begins as white light—full of raw potential, experience, and technical skills. But leadership is not about staying plain. It's about refracting that potential through the prism of **Knowledge, Skills, and Attitude** to emerge as a spectrum of seven competencies (VIBGYOR). This is your personal transformation.

2. **Stage Two: Act as a Prism for Others**

Once you embody these colours, you become a prism for your team. Your role is to empower, coach, and instil these competencies in others. This is how leadership moves from being a title to becoming a culture.

Section B: Why Refraction Matters

- Organisational impact.

Why Refraction Matters

Refraction is not just a change—it's an **intentional transformation**. It means bending old habits, challenging comfort zones, and creating clarity. Without refraction:

- Leaders remain stuck in operational tasks.
- Teams stay dependent.
- Organisations fail to innovate and grow.

With refraction

- Leaders evolve into catalysts.
- Teams become autonomous and confident.
- Organisations thrive in a competitive world.

"VMPL's leadership challenge was not about lack of experience—it was about lack of adaptability. Managers were stuck in operational silos, resisting digital change, and creating dependency within teams. Attrition was high, and customer complaints were increasing. When VMPL set an ambitious goal to grow turnover by 35%, it became clear that leadership transformation was the key. This is where the Prism Framework came into play."

How Leaders and Organisations Create Transformation

Transformation begins with clarity and commitment:

- Leaders **develop themselves first** by adopting the seven colours of leadership.

- Organisations **support this journey** by creating systems for assessment, coaching, and accountability.
- When leaders act as prisms, they cascade these competencies to their teams, creating a culture of empowerment and growth.

VMPL Example

Why VMPL needed transformation

- Traditional processes (paper trails, low digital adoption).
- High attrition (31%).
- Leadership promotions based on tenure/performance, not capability.
- Customer complaints are piling up due to poor communication and dependency.

What triggered the change

- Ananya's observations in customer care.
- Leadership gaps identified during internal review.
- Organisational goal to increase turnover by 35%.

VMPL realised that leadership gaps were causing high attrition and poor customer experience. By focusing on coaching (Orange) and decision-making (Yellow), they began to reduce dependency and improve team confidence.

Mapping Skills to Colours and Assigning Numerical Values

To make transformation measurable

- Each colour represents a **competency** linked to leadership skills.
- Use the **Prism Matrix** to assign numerical values:
  - **0** = No capability demonstrated
  - **1** = Very low capability
  - **2** = Basic capability
  - **3** = Moderate capability
  - **4** = Strong capability
  - **5** = Excellent / Role model capability
- Assess both **leader and team scores** for each colour.
- Calculate the **Refraction Index:**

$$\text{Refraction Index} = \frac{\text{Current Score}}{\text{Target Score}} \times 100\%$$

What Happens After Scoring?

Once you calculate the Refraction Index and identify gaps:

1. **Prioritise Competencies**
   - Use gap analysis to decide which colours need immediate attention.

- **Example:** Gap ≥ 3 → Immediate coaching; Gap = 1–2 → Enhance; Gap = 0 → Monitor.

2. **Link to Development Actions**
    - Immediate Attention → Short-term interventions (coaching, mentoring).
    - Enhance → Medium-term plans (training, workshops).
    - Monitor → Recognition and reinforcement.
3. **Create an Action Plan**
    - Move from interpretation to implementation using templates (Chapter 6).
    - **Example:** Orange scored 1 → Action plan includes weekly coaching sessions and delegation exercises.
4. **Track Progress Over Time**
    - Use Refraction Index as a benchmark.
    - **Example:** Initial Index = 50%, target = 90% in 3 months.

Now that we have understood the refraction strategy, it is essential to examine the practical movement of the stages involved. This section will help us gain a deeper understanding of how we can bring the accuracy and ensure no faults.

Section C: The Four Steps

- Self-assessment.
- Set development goals.
- Empower team.
- Monitor progress.

Step 1: Self-Assessment

- Understand where you stand today.

How: Use the **Prism Matrix** to evaluate your current vs. target scores for each colour.

Part 1: Self-Assessment (Leader's Own Competency)

Behavioural Anchors for Scoring (0–5 scale)

- **0:** Never demonstrates the behaviour.
- **1:** Rarely demonstrates the behaviour.
- **2:** Occasionally demonstrates the behaviour.
- **3:** Frequently demonstrates the behaviour.

- **4:** Consistently demonstrates the behaviour.
- **5:** Role model for the behaviour.

Questions

- Do you actively mentor or coach team members for career growth?
- How often do you conduct structured performance reviews?
- Do you recognise and reward team contributions regularly?
- Do you manage underperformance with clear action plans?

Sample Scoring (VMPL Leader)

Question	Score
Mentoring team members	2
Conducting performance reviews	3
Recognizing contributions	2
Managing underperformance	1
Average Score	2 → Needs Enhancement

Universal Questions

These are behaviour-based questions for each competency (provided in the appendix). They ensure consistency and objectivity.

Example: VMPL managers scored low on Orange (People Management) and Green (Innovation), indicating dependency and resistance to change.

Step 2: Set Development Goals

- Identify gaps and prioritise actions:
    - Gap ≥ 3 → Immediate Attention
    - Gap = 1–2 → Enhance
    - Gap = 0 → Monitor
- **Example:** VMPL prioritised coaching and decision-making first.

Step 3: Empower Your Team

- Assess team scores using the same matrix.
- Share feedback and create mentoring plans.
- Delegate responsibilities gradually to reduce dependency.
- **Example:** VMPL introduced weekly coaching sessions for team leads.

Step 4: Monitor Progress

- Track improvement using scores and Refraction Index.
- Review progress monthly or quarterly.

- Celebrate milestones and adjust strategies.
- **Example:** VMPL reduced dependency by 20% in three months.

Section D: Tools for Implementation

- Prism Matrix.
- Refraction Index.
- Universal questions (background).

1. **Prism Matrix Overview**
   - A structured assessment tool mapping competencies to colours and scores.
   - **Used for**
     - Individual assessment.
     - Team benchmarking.

Example: VMPL used the Prism Matrix to identify gaps in Orange (People Management) and Yellow (Decision-Making).

2. **Refraction Index Formula**

$$\text{Refraction Index} = \frac{\text{Current Score}}{\text{Target Score}} \times 100\%$$

➢ **Why it matters**

- Tracks progress over time.
- Creates accountability.

➢ **Example**

- Current Score = 2, Target Score = 4 → Refraction Index = 50%.

3. Universal Question Background

➢ **Why it matters**

- Ensures fairness and consistency.
- Behaviour-based, not opinion-based.

➢ The full question set is provided in the appendix for easy reference.

4. Dashboard Concept for Visual Clarity

The Leadership Spectrum Dashboard converts complex data into visuals: (you will get a pictorial representation in chapter 5)

- **Colour Spectrum Bar:** Shows progress for each competency.
- **Radial Chart:** Displays gaps at a glance.
- **Heatmap Table:** Highlights organisational trends.
- **Action Summary Panel:** Lists top priorities and suggested actions.

Why it matters

- **Clarity:** Converts numbers into visuals.
- **Focus:** Highlights priority areas.
- **Benchmarking:** Enables comparison across leaders and teams.
- **Tracking:** Supports progress monitoring over time.

Section E: Closing Reflection

Who Uses This Strategy?

The Refraction Strategy is not just for individual leaders—it's a framework that involves multiple stakeholders:

1. Leaders for Self-Assessment

Leaders use the Prism Matrix to evaluate their own competencies and identify development areas. However, self-assessment can be biased**. To ensure accuracy:**

- Combine self-assessment with **360-degree feedback** from peers, subordinates, and supervisors.
- Use **behavioural anchors** for scoring to make assessments objective.
- Validate responses through HR review or digital tools that require evidence of actions.

2. HR for Talent Development

HR plays a critical role in embedding this strategy into organisational culture:

- Use Prism Matrix scores to design **personalised development plans**.
- Align low-scoring competencies with **training programs and coaching interventions**.
- Integrate Prism assessments into **performance reviews** to reinforce leadership behaviours.

- Support **succession planning** by identifying high-potential employees based on Prism scores.

3. Organisations for Leadership Benchmarking

Organisations can leverage the Prism Framework for

- **Hiring:** Benchmark candidates for leadership roles against organisational standards.
- **HR Operations:** Embed Prism assessments into HRMS for leadership pipeline tracking and progress dashboards.
- **Culture Building:** Use aggregated data to identify systemic gaps and design interventions.

Leadership is a continuous 'refraction' process. When leaders transform themselves and act as prisms for their teams, they create a ripple effect—empowered individuals, stronger teams, and organisations that thrive in the face of change.

Reflection Questions

- Which gaps in your Prism Matrix need immediate attention?
- How will you use the Refraction Index to track progress?
- Who all will you involve in your leadership development journey?
- What old habits or comfort zones do you need to bend to create transformation?

- How will you measure your leadership impact beyond KPIs?
- What is that one immediate action you can take to start refraction?

"Strategy needs structure. Let's turn ideas into measurable actions using the Prism Matrix."

Chapter - 5
The Prism Matrix

In Chapter 4, we explored the concept of dual transformation—leaders first refract their own potential into a spectrum of competencies and then act as prisms for their teams.

However, transformation requires more than just intent; it necessitates a practical method for measuring and tracking progress. This is where the Prism Matrix comes in. It turns leadership development from an abstract idea into a structured, measurable process. For VMPL, this tool became the starting point for change, helping them identify gaps, prioritise actions, and benchmark leadership capability across the organisation.

Section A: Practical Tool for Assessment and Development

- **Section 1:** VMPL Context – The Turning Point
- **Section 2:** What is the Prism Matrix and How It Works
- **Section 3:** How the Assessment Was Conducted (with scoring logic and sample questionnaire)

Section 1: VMPL Context – The Turning Point

Now we know many things about VMPL—Versatile Manufacturing Pvt. Ltd. Like most organisations, it started with a clear aim: to grow, earn profits, and build a strong reputation. In Chapter 4, we saw how VMPL's managers began to understand their development areas and how they could act as prisms for others. That was the essence of the Refraction Strategy—leaders transforming themselves and enabling their teams.

But here's what happened next: when VMPL leaders first saw their scores, the reaction was mixed. Some rejected the results outright, saying, "We've been doing this for years—how can we score so low?" Others accepted the facts and were ready to work on improvement. This resistance was natural—change is never easy.

Does this happen in your organisation as well? When feedback or assessment reveals gaps, do people embrace it or resist it?

What changed the conversation at VMPL was the Prism Matrix. It didn't just show numbers—it showed **clarity**. Leaders could see exactly which competencies were holding them back and how improving them would impact their teams and the organisation. The tool was transparent, objective, and actionable.

It gave leaders a roadmap for development and made progress measurable. That's why even those who resisted initially began to accept the process.

Section 2: What is the Prism Matrix and How It Works

The Prism Matrix is a practical tool for assessment and development. It turns leadership transformation into a structured, measurable process. Here's how it works:

➢ **Mapping Skills to Colours**

Each leadership competency is linked to a colour in the VIBGYOR spectrum. For example:

- **Violet** = Vision & Strategic Thinking
- **Orange** = People Management & Coaching

  This mapping makes it easy to visualise and prioritise development areas.

➢ **Assigning Numerical Values**

Leaders and teams answer universal questions (provided in the appendix) for each competency. Based on responses, scores are assigned on a scale of 0–5:

- **0** = No capability demonstrated
- **5** = Excellent / Role model capability

➢ **Identifying Gaps**

The matrix compares the current score vs. the target score for each competency. The difference (gap) shows where development is needed.

Larger gaps = higher priority.

➢ Benchmarking Performance

By aggregating scores across leaders or departments, organisations can:

- Spot trends (e.g., low Orange = weak people management culture).
- Compare leaders for succession planning.
- Track progress over time using the Refraction Index:

$$\text{Refraction Index} = \frac{\text{Current Score}}{\text{Target Score}} \times 100\%$$

This process ensures clarity, fairness, and accountability—making leadership development a measurable journey rather than a **vague concept.**

Section 3: How the assessment was conducted

VMPL used a universal question set for each competency. Each question was behaviour-based and rated on a scale of 0 to 5. For example:

Orange – People Management & Coaching

- How often do you delegate responsibilities effectively?
- Do you conduct regular coaching sessions for team members?
- Do you empower team members to make decisions?

Scoring

- **0** = Never
- **5** = Always

Sample Snapshot for Orange (People Management)

Question	Score
How often do you delegate responsibilities effectively?	1
Do you conduct regular coaching sessions for team members?	2
Do you empower team members to make decisions?	1
Average Score	**1.3 → Rounded to 1**

This score was then entered into the Prism Matrix alongside target scores.

Section B: Individual and Team Examples

- **Section 4:** Individual Example (Rajesh – Plant Head at VMPL)
- **Section 5:** Team Example (VMPL Sales Department)

Section 4: Individual Example (VMPL Leader)

Here's how the Prism Matrix looked for one VMPL manager:'

Color	Competency	Leader Current Score	Leader Target Score	Priority
Violet	Vision & Strategic Thinking	4	4	Monitor
Indigo	Integrity & Ethics	4	5	Enhance
Blue	Communication & Influence	2	4	Enhance
Green	Growth & Innovation	1	3	Enhance
Yellow	Decision-Making & Problem Solving	2	4	Immediate
Orange	People Management & Coaching	1	4	Immediate
Red	Execution & Results Orientation	3	5	Enhance

Interpretation

- Immediate focus on Orange (People Management), Yellow (Decision-Making), and Red (Execution).
- **Enhance:** Green (Innovation), Blue (Communication), Indigo (Integrity and Ethics)
- **Monitor:** Violet (Strategic thinking or Initiatives)

Interpretation and Action

When a leader sees their Prism Matrix scores, the next step is to interpret and act. For example, if a leader scores **1 on Orange (People Management)**, this signals **Immediate Attention**.

Action Plan

- Schedule weekly coaching sessions with team members.
- Delegate at least two responsibilities within the next month.
- Create a mentoring plan for high-potential employees.

Priority Coding Application

- Gap $\geq 3 \rightarrow$ Immediate Attention
- Gap = 1–2 $\rightarrow$ Enhance
- Gap = 0 $\rightarrow$ Monitor

Refraction Index Tracking

If the current score is 1 and the target is 4, the Refraction Index is:

$$\text{Refraction Index} = \frac{1}{4} \times 100\% = 25\%$$

This becomes the baseline for progress tracking.

Section 5: Team Example (VMPL Department)

Aggregated scores for a VMPL department:

Color	Competency	Team Avg Current Score	Team Target Score	Priority
Violet	Vision & Strategic Thinking	1.5	3	Enhance
Indigo	Integrity & Ethics	2.5	4	Enhance
Blue	Communication & Influence	2	4	Enhance
Green	Growth & Innovation	1	3	Enhance
Yellow	Decision-Making & Problem Solving	1.8	4	Immediate

Orange	People Management & Coaching	1.2	3.5	Immediate
Red	Execution & Results Orientation	2.5	4.5	Immediate

Interpretation

- **Organisational trend:** Low scores in Orange and Yellow indicate dependency and slow decision-making.
- Green (Innovation) also needs attention to support digital transformation.

Organizational Insights

Aggregated team scores reveal cultural gaps. For example, VMPL's Sales team scored **low on Blue (Communication)**, indicating a need for collaboration workshops and structured communication channels.

HR Action Points

- Design team-level training programs for communication and influence.
- Introduce monthly cross-functional meetings to improve collaboration.
- Monitor improvement through team-level Prism Matrix updates.

Section C: How to use it for leadership benchmarking

- **Section 6:** Why This Builds Trust – And Why It Works for Organisations

  (Expanded with benefits like cultural clarity, reducing resistance, succession planning, engagement, and accountability)

- **Section 7:** Leadership Spectrum Dashboard (Pictorial Guide + Interpretation Steps)

Section 6: Leadership Benchmarking

One reason VMPL leaders eventually accepted the Prism Matrix was trust. The process was transparent, objective, and fair. It wasn't about judgment—it was about growth.

Every score was backed by clear questions and measurable actions, making development a shared responsibility rather than a top-down mandate.

Why should organisations adopt this method?

- **Creates a Culture of Clarity:** Everyone knows what leadership means and how it's measured. So, they are not talking leadership as a concept or some designation, but the term is seriously getting ingrained in their organisational culture.
- **Reduces Resistance to Change:** "Resistance to change often stems from bias and lack of clarity in assessments. When leadership assessments are transparent, fair, and backed by clear criteria, leaders are more likely to accept feedback. The Prism Matrix ensures this transparency by linking scores to measurable behaviours, making the need for change clear and meaningful. This depth

helps leaders understand why change is necessary and how it benefits them and the organisation."

- **Links Development to Business Goals:** By focusing on competencies that matter (Vision, Execution, People Management), organisations align leadership growth with strategic priorities. Hence, developments are not vague targets or some vision without direction. It is a strategic plan with direction. Each competency directly aligns with organisational goals. This gives measurable business impacts.
- **Improves Succession Planning:** In many organisations, planning is just known as a concept. The HR team knows the concept, but making it work could be a task. Benchmarking across leaders helps identify high-potential talent and close gaps early. With the Prism Matrix, it becomes part of the culture. Benchmarking leaders creates enthusiasm for building a future-ready team and ensures continuity in critical roles.
- **Drives Engagement and Retention:** Engagement isn't just about rewards or annual events. It's about meaningful growth. Celebrating milestones after successful development plans creates positivity. High performers stay because they see progress; those unwilling to adapt naturally exit—strengthening the team.

Employees feel supported when development is structured and measurable, reducing attrition.

- **Builds Accountability:** The Refraction Index introduces seriousness into leadership development. It's not about vague feedback—it's about measurable progress. Leaders and organisations can track growth over time, making accountability a shared responsibility. Progress is tracked through the Refraction Index, making leadership development a continuous process.

VMPL's experience proved this: once leaders understood the logic and saw progress, they became advocates for the process. Imagine the impact if your organisation embraced this approach—clear expectations, measurable growth, and a leadership pipeline ready for the future.

Section 7: Leadership Spectrum Dashboard

To make interpretation easier, the **Leadership Spectrum Dashboard** converts the Prism Matrix into a visual format:

The **Leadership Spectrum Dashboard** is designed to make the Prism Matrix easy to interpret and visually appealing. It provides leaders and organisations with a clear snapshot of where they stand and what actions are needed

1. **Header Section**
    - Displays the leader's name or department.
    - Shows the Refraction Index (overall progress percentage).

- Includes the date of assessment for tracking over time.

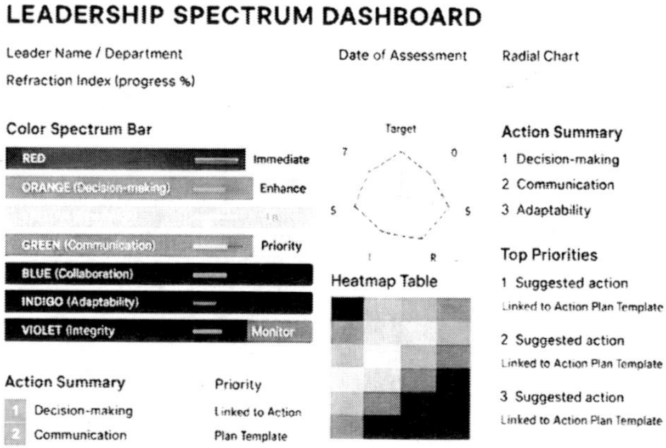

2. Colour Spectrum Bar

- A horizontal bar representing the seven colours (VIBGYOR).
- Each colour segment includes:
  - Competency Name (e.g., Vision, Integrity, Communication).
  - Current Score vs. Target Score displayed as a progress bar.
  - Priority Tag (Immediate, Enhance, Monitor) for quick action planning.

3. Individual Leader View

- A radial chart (spider graph) plotting all seven competencies.
- Shows gaps between current and target scores visually.

- Helps leaders identify their strongest and weakest areas at a glance.

4. **Team View**
   - A heatmap table showing aggregated scores for each competency across team members or departments.
   - Darker shades indicate bigger gaps, making organisational trends easy to spot.

5. **Action Summary Panel**
   - Lists the Top 3 Priority Areas for the leader or team.
   - Suggests next steps linked to the Action Plan Template in the appendix

Why This Dashboard Matters

- **Clarity:** Converts complex data into simple visuals.
- **Focus:** Highlights priority areas for immediate action.
- **Benchmarking:** Enables comparison across leaders and teams.
- **Tracking:** Supports progress monitoring over time.

"The Prism Matrix turns leadership development from a concept into a measurable journey. Combined with the Leadership Spectrum Dashboard, it gives leaders and organisations the clarity they need to act. In the next section, we'll explore templates and tools to make implementation seamless."

HR Integration and System Embedding

Leadership transformation cannot succeed if it remains a standalone initiative. To make it sustainable, HR must embed the Prism Framework into organisational systems. This ensures leadership development becomes measurable, continuous, and aligned with business goals.

Why HR Integration Matters?

HR is the custodian of talent strategy. When leadership assessments are linked to HR operations:

- Leadership development moves from reactive training to strategic capability building.
- Progress becomes visible and trackable through dashboards.
- Development plans align with succession planning and organisational growth.

Actionable Steps for HR Integration

1. **Embed Prism Matrix into HRMS**
    - Integrate Prism scores into HR systems for real-time visibility.
    - Assign ownership: HR for tracking, managers for execution.

2. **Automate Alerts**
    - Set triggers for competencies needing immediate attention.
    - **Example:** If the Orange (People Management) score < 2, HR receives an alert to initiate coaching.
3. **Link Prism Scores to LMS**
    - Map low-scoring competencies to targeted learning modules.
    - **Example:** Leaders scoring low on Blue (Communication) automatically enrolled in influence workshops.
4. **Create Leadership Dashboards**
    - Visualise leadership health across departments.
    - Include Refraction Index trends for individuals and teams.

Recruitment and Succession Planning

Benchmarking through Prism ensures organisations hire leaders who align with cultural and competency expectations.

Actionable Steps by HR Team

1. **Include Prism Assessment in Leadership Hiring**
    - Candidates complete Prism-based evaluation during recruitment.
    - Compare scores against organisational benchmarks.

2. **Use Benchmarking for Succession**
    - Identify high-potential employees for future roles.
    - **Example:** Employees with strong Red (Execution) and Violet (Vision) scores are shortlisted for strategic roles.

VMPL Example

When VMPL integrated Prism into recruitment and succession planning, the HR Head said:

"Now we hire for leadership readiness, not just experience."

They identified managers with strong Red (Execution) scores for future Plant Head roles and created coaching plans for those with gaps in Violet (Vision). This approach ensured leadership continuity and reduced dependency on external hires.

Reflection Questions

- Which gaps in your Prism Matrix need immediate attention?
- How will you use the Refraction Index to track progress?
- Who will you involve in your leadership development journey?

"You've seen how to assess leadership. Now, let's embed this into your organisation for real impact."

Chapter - 6
Organisational Application

Using the Prism for

- Leadership pipeline development.
- Succession planning.
- Cost optimisation through skill mapping.

➢ **Group vs. individual implementation.**

Leadership transformation at VMPL didn't stop at individual assessments. Once the Prism Matrix revealed gaps in competencies, the next challenge was embedding these insights into the organisation's systems. VMPL realised that leadership development could no longer be an isolated activity—it had to become part of the organisational DNA.

Initially, VMPL's approach was reactive: managers attended training programs without a clear link to business goals. This resulted in inconsistent outcomes and wasted resources. The Prism Framework changed that by providing a structured, measurable way to align leadership development with organisational strategy.

HR took the lead in this transformation. Using Prism Matrix scores, they designed targeted interventions instead of generic programs. They created a **leadership pipeline**, implemented **succession planning for critical roles**, and optimised costs by focusing only on the competencies that mattered most. For VMPL, this was a turning point—leadership development became a strategic enabler rather than a checkbox activity.

In this chapter, we will explore how organisations can replicate VMPL's success by

- Embedding the Prism Framework into HR and operational systems.
- Using Prism scores for **leadership pipeline development**, **succession planning**, and **cost optimisation**.
- Implementing the framework at both the **individual and group levels**.
- Leveraging **digital tools and dashboards** for real-time tracking.
- Driving engagement and retention through structured recognition.

Section 1: Why Organisational Application Matters

Leadership development is often treated as a training activity, disconnected from business strategy. This approach fails because leadership is not just about skills—it's about driving organisational goals. When leadership development is aligned with business strategy, it becomes a powerful enabler for growth, innovation, and cultural transformation.

I have been working in the Learning & Development field for over 15 years. Many times, I hear organisations say:

"This is the missing skill—give them the training," or "This person needs communication skills training."

As a consultant, I always suggest that training is not the only solution. There could be more effective ways to achieve the desired results. Leadership development should never become a **checkbox activity**, nor should organisations conclude that training alone will solve performance gaps. Instead, we need structured tools that diagnose the real issues and provide actionable strategies.

The **Prism Framework** solves this by making leadership development measurable, actionable, and scalable. It connects individual growth to organisational priorities, ensuring that every leadership intervention contributes to business outcomes.

Let us look into the VMPL Example

VMPL initially relied on traditional training programs without linking them to strategic needs. Managers attended workshops, but the impact was unclear. After adopting the Prism Framework, VMPL shifted to a system-driven approach:

- HR used Prism Matrix scores to design targeted interventions.
- Leadership development became part of succession planning and pipeline building.
- Training costs were optimised by focusing only on critical competencies.

This transformation turned leadership development from a checkbox activity into a strategic advantage.

Section 2: Using the Prism for Strategic Goals

After VMPL completed its leadership assessments, the HR Head sat in a review meeting, looking at the dashboard filled with colourful scores. She said,

"This is more than fixing gaps—this is about building a company where leadership drives everything."

Until now, leadership development at VMPL has been reactive: a training here, a workshop there, often triggered by performance issues or feedback from managers. But the Prism Framework changed the game. It gave VMPL a way to **see leadership as a system**, not an isolated activity. For the first time, they could identify future leaders, prepare successors, and optimise resources—all while aligning with business strategy.

This was the moment VMPL started its journey to become a **leadership-powered organisation**—an organisation where leadership is not just a role but a culture embedded at every level.

Developing Future Leaders (Leadership Pipeline)

Empty spaces in the organisational chart aren't just vacancies—they're opportunities to groom internal talent. The Prism Matrix helps identify who's ready and who needs development.

- **How It Works**
  - Assess all managers using the Prism Matrix.
  - Identify those scoring high on Violet (Vision) and Red (Execution) for future leadership roles.
  - Create tiered development programs for these employees.

- **VMPL Example**

VMPL used Prism scores to shortlist five managers for future Plant Head roles. These managers were enrolled in advanced leadership programs focused on strategic thinking and innovation.

Succession Planning

Succession planning often fails because it's reactive. The Prism Framework makes it proactive by benchmarking leaders against organisational standards.

- **How It Works**
  - Use Prism Matrix during performance reviews.
  - Compare current leaders' scores with target benchmarks for critical roles.
  - Design coaching plans for gaps in competencies like Orange (People Management) or Yellow (Decision-Making).

- **VMPL Example**
  - VMPL identified that two senior managers lacked strategic vision (Violet). HR created a six-month coaching plan before considering them for higher roles.

Cost Optimisation through Skill Mapping

Generic training programs waste resources. Prism Matrix enables targeted interventions by mapping skills to actual gaps.

- **How It Works**
  - Aggregate team scores to identify common gaps.
  - Focus training budgets on competencies with the largest gaps.
- **VMPL Example**
  - Instead of running broad leadership workshops, VMPL invested in specialised programs for Orange (People Management) and Blue (Communication), reducing training costs by 30%.

Section 3: Group vs. Individual Implementation

The Prism Framework is designed to be flexible—it can be applied at both **individual** and **group levels**, depending on the organisation's needs. VMPL's experience shows how these two approaches complement each other to create a leadership-powered culture.

Individual Implementation

Individual implementation focuses on personalised development plans based on Prism Matrix scores.

- **How It Works**
  - Each leader completes the Prism assessment.
  - Scores are analysed to identify gaps and create tailored action plans.
  - Progress is tracked using the Refraction Index.
- **VMPL Scenario**
  - Rajesh, Plant Head, scored low on Orange (People Management). His action plan included weekly coaching sessions and delegation exercises. Within three months, his Refraction Index improved from 25% to 70%, and his team reported higher autonomy and engagement.

Group Implementation

Group implementation addresses cultural and systemic gaps by analysing aggregated team scores.

- **How It Works**
  - Assess entire departments or teams using the Prism Matrix.
  - Identify common gaps across the group.
  - Design interventions like workshops, cross-functional projects, or leadership boot camps.
- **VMPL Scenario**
  - VMPL's Sales team scored low on Blue (Communication) and Green (Innovation). HR organised monthly collaboration workshops and launched an "Innovation Challenge" to encourage creative problem-solving. Within six months, team scores improved by 40%, and cross-functional collaboration became a norm.

Why Both Approaches Matter

- **Individual Implementation** builds **personal leadership capability**.
- **Group Implementation** strengthens **the organisational culture.**

  Together, they create a leadership-powered organisation where leadership is not just a role but a shared responsibility.

Section 4: HR Integration and Digital Tools

When VMPL completed its leadership assessments, the HR team gathered around the dashboard for the first time. The screen was filled with colours—Violet, Orange, Red—each telling a story about their managers. The HR Head leaned back and said,

"For years, we've been guessing who's ready for the next role. Now, we can see it clearly."

Until then, leadership development at VMPL was reactive. A manager struggled with communication. Send them to a workshop. Someone missed targets? Enroll them in a training program. But these fixes were short-lived because they didn't address the root cause. The Prism Framework changed that. It gave HR a way to **embed leadership development into the organisation's DNA**.

Making It Part of the System

The first step was integration. VMPL's HR team linked the Prism Matrix to their HRMS. This meant:

- Every manager's scores were visible in real time.
- Alerts popped up when a competency needed immediate attention.

- Training programs in the LMS were mapped to specific gaps.

No more generic workshops. No more guesswork. Development became **data-driven and personalised**.

Why Digital Tools Matter

Digital dashboards have made leadership health tangible. HR could:

- Track progress through the **Refraction Index**.
- Compare departments to spot cultural gaps.
- Plan succession with confidence.

One HR manager said,

"This isn't just a dashboard—it's a leadership map. We know who's ready, who needs help, and where the future leaders are."

Becoming a Leadership-Powered Organisation

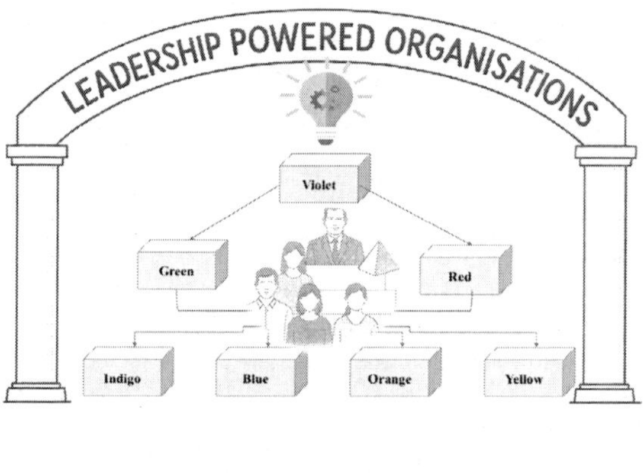

This integration wasn't just about technology—it was about transformation. VMPL moved from being a company that reacted to problems to one that **built**

leaders proactively. Leadership became a strategic advantage, not a checkbox activity. And that's what makes an organisation truly **leadership-powered**.

Reflection Questions

- How does your organisation currently approach leadership development—reactive or strategic?
- Which system (HRMS, LMS, dashboards) can you integrate with the Prism Framework?
- What is one organisational process you will embed leadership behaviours into?

"Embedding leadership is powerful—but how do we prove impact? Let's connect leadership behaviours to business results."

Chapter - 7
Driving Organisational Impact Through Results

How VMPL Created the Impact

When VMPL completed its Prism assessments, the leadership team gathered to review the dashboard. The screen displayed colourful scores—Violet for vision, Orange for people management, Red for execution. The HR Head broke the silence:

"We've got the data. But how do we turn this into real impact?"

Until now, leadership development has been measured by attendance in training programs or feedback forms. But the Prism Framework changed the conversation. It wasn't about ticking boxes anymore—it was about connecting leadership behaviours to business outcomes. This chapter explores how organisations can move from **data to decisions** and create measurable impact.

Section A: From Data to Decisions

Data without action is just numbers. The Prism Matrix provides clarity, but organisations need to translate these insights into decisions that shape performance and culture.

➢ **Why This Matters**

- Leadership scores reveal more than individual gaps—they highlight systemic issues. For example, if multiple managers score low on Yellow (Decision-Making), it signals a risk for operational delays.

➢ **How to Use It**

- Identify patterns in aggregated scores.
- Link leadership gaps to business challenges.
- Prioritise interventions based on strategic impact.

➢ **VMPL Example**

- VMPL noticed that several managers scored low on Orange (People Management). This explained why teams were overly dependent on their leaders, slowing down decision-making. HR decided to launch a coaching initiative focused on delegation and empowerment, reducing bottlenecks and improving productivity.

Section B: Embedding Results into Business Processes

Leadership development cannot succeed if it remains outside the business framework. To make it real, organisations must embed leadership behaviours into KPIs, performance reviews, and career progression. This is where Prism results become powerful—they move from dashboards to decisions.

When VMPL realised that Orange (People Management) was a critical gap, they knew this wasn't just about coaching—it had to become part of how the organisation operated. During a leadership review, the HR Head said:

"If we want managers to empower their teams, it should reflect in their KPIs and career progression."

And that's exactly what they did.

How VMPL Embedded Orange into Processes

- **Performance Reviews**

  Managers were evaluated not only on operational results but also on how effectively they developed their teams. A new metric was added: *"Team Autonomy Score."*

- **Promotions and Role Assignments**

  Leadership readiness was benchmarked using Prism scores. Managers with strong orange scores were prioritised for roles requiring people leadership.

- **Training and Development**

  Instead of generic workshops, VMPL introduced targeted coaching programs linked to Prism gaps.

Let us understand the same for Green and Red colours

- **Green – Growth & Innovation**

  Innovation was a strategic priority for VMPL, but Prism results showed low scores on Green. HR embedded an *Innovation Contribution Metric* into KPIs, rewarding managers who encouraged creative solutions and implemented process improvements.

- **Red – Execution & Results Orientation**

  Execution gaps were impacting delivery timelines. VMPL introduced a *Leadership Execution Index* that combined operational KPIs with Prism scores. Managers who consistently met targets and demonstrated structured execution behaviours were recognised and fast-tracked for critical roles.

Turning Leadership Insights into Business Rules

Embedding results into business processes ensures leadership development is not a side activity—it becomes part of the organisational DNA. When KPIs, promotions, and rewards reflect leadership behaviours, managers take ownership of their growth. **This is how organisations move from training-driven development to becoming leadership-powered companies.**

Section C: Measuring Organisational Impact

When VMPL rolled out the Prism Framework, the leadership team didn't just want colourful dashboards—they wanted proof that these changes were making a difference. The CEO asked during a quarterly review:

"We've invested time and effort. How do we know it's working?"

That question is at the heart of this section. Measuring impact isn't about guesswork—it's about connecting leadership development to tangible business outcomes.

How to Measure Impact Practically

1. **Track Refraction Index Over Time**
   - Calculate the Refraction Index for each leader and team:

$$\text{Refraction Index} = \frac{\text{Current Score}}{\text{Target Score}} \times 100\%$$

   - **Example:** A manager's Orange score improved from 1 to 3 (Target = 4) → Refraction Index jumped from 25% to 75%.

2. **Compare Pre- and Post-Implementation Results**
   - **Before Prism:** VMPL had high dependency and slow decision-making.
   - **After Prism:** Team autonomy scores improved by 40%, and project turnaround time reduced by 15%.

3. **Link Leadership Metrics to Business KPIs**
    - Orange (People Management) → Employee engagement scores.
    - Red (Execution) → On-time delivery rates.
    - Green (Innovation) → Number of new ideas implemented.
4. **Use Dashboards for Visibility**
    - Leadership health dashboards show progress at individual, team, and organisational levels.
    - VMPL's HR team used these dashboards to identify departments improving fastest and those needing extra support.

"Proving Impact: From Leadership Scores to Business Outcomes"

When leadership development is measured, it becomes credible. It moves from being a "soft initiative" to a strategic lever for performance. VMPL didn't just see better scores—they saw faster decisions, stronger teams, and reduced costs. That's the true impact of the Prism Framework.

Reflection Questions

- How will you link leadership behaviours to business KPIs in your organisation?
- Which metric (Engagement, Autonomy, Innovation) matters most for your growth?
- What cultural shift will prove that leadership development is working?

"Theory meets reality. Here are case studies showing how organisations applied the Prism Framework."

Chapter - 8
Case Studies & Scenarios

Disclaimer

The case studies presented in this chapter are intended for educational and illustrative purposes. They are inspired by real-world scenarios but adapted to demonstrate the application of the Prism Framework. Names, data, and situations have been modified to protect confidentiality and to focus on leadership concepts rather than specific organisational details.

The Prism Framework is not just a theory—it works across industries. Why? Because this tool focuses on leaders—the people who drive business outcomes every day. It's a deep dive into the competencies that shape decisions, influence culture, and deliver results.

In this chapter, we'll explore real-world issues, real situations, and real results through the Prism lens. From FMCG to Pharma, Automotive to Retail, these case studies will show how organisations used the Prism approach to solve leadership challenges and transform their business performance.

How will you read the case studies?

1. **Look for the Context:** Understand the industry and organisational challenges. Ask yourself a question: Do we face any of these issues? Or do I want to place my organisational or individual challenges here?

2. **Focus on the assessment**: Notice how The Prism Matrix is applied, the scores for each competency and the refraction index. This primarily shows the leadership gap.

3. **Interpret the actions:** Look for how the organisation linked Prism insights to business process- KPIs, training, and cultural shifts

4. **Analyse the outcomes:** Pay attention to measurable results like improved forecasting, reduced attrition, or faster decision-making. These outcomes demonstrate the ROI of leadership development

5. **Apply the key takeaways:** Each case ends with a takeaway. Reflect on how these lessons can be adapted to your organisation.

FMCG Case Study: Transforming Leadership for Business Agility

Story Context

An FMCG company, a household name for decades, was struggling to keep pace with market dynamics. The second-generation owner had recently taken charge, supported by a board of experienced directors. But the culture remained **owner-driven**, slowing decisions and innovation.

The business challenges were mounting

- **250 SKUs** created complexity in forecasting.
- Products were priced **12% higher than competitors**, forcing distributors to invest **₹15–20 lakh per outlet**.
- **Sales targets had increased by 18% year-on-year**, creating pressure across the network.
- **Forecasting accuracy dropped to 65%**, leading to material wastage worth **₹2 crore annually**.

The leadership team knew something had to change—and fast.

Prism Assessment

The company introduced the **Prism Framework** to diagnose leadership gaps. Assessments were conducted for 40 managers across sales, supply chain, and operations using universal questions for all seven colours.

Sample Questions Used in Assessment

- **Violet (Vision):** *Do you set long-term goals for your department?*
- **Indigo (Integrity):** *Do you maintain transparency in decision-making?*
- **Blue (Communication):** *Do you adapt your communication style for different audiences?*

- **Green (Innovation):** *Do you encourage your team to propose new ideas?*
- **Yellow (Decision-Making):** *Do you make decisions based on data rather than assumptions?*
- **Orange (People Management):** *Do you actively mentor team members for career growth?*
- **Red (Execution):** *Do you monitor progress against goals regularly?*

Here's a snapshot of three key leaders

Target Score for all colours: 4

Leader Name	Violet	Indigo	Blue	Green	Yellow	Orange	Red	Target Score- 4 for all colours	Refraction Index
Rajesh (Plant Head)	3	4	2	2	3	1	3	28	64.3
Meera (Sales Head)	2	4	3	1	2	2	3	28	60.7
Anil (Supply Chain)	3	3	2	2	2	1	4	28	60.7

Interpretation

- **Orange (People Management)** was the weakest across all leaders (avg. score = 1.8).
- **Green (Growth & Innovation)** scored low (avg. score = 2.0), signalling a lack of creativity in SKU rationalisation and forecasting.
- **Red (Execution)** was moderate but needed improvement for timely delivery.

Implementation

Based on Prism insights

- **Orange:** Introduced coaching programs for managers and embedded the *Team Autonomy Score* in KPIs.
- **Green:** Launched an "Innovation Sprint" to rationalise SKUs and improve forecasting.
- **Red:** Added *Leadership Execution Index* to performance reviews, linking operational KPIs with leadership behaviours.

HR integrated Prism dashboards into their HRMS, enabling real-time tracking of Refraction Index for each manager.

The Outcome

Within six months

- Forecasting accuracy improved from **65% to 83%**, reducing material wastage by **₹1.2 crore**.
- SKU rationalisation cut redundant products by **12%**, easing distributor investment pressure.
- Sales team engagement scores improved by **22%**, reducing attrition.
- Leadership culture began shifting from **owner-driven to system-driven**, creating agility.

Key Takeaway

The Prism Framework helped the FMCG company move from reactive fixes to a structured leadership strategy. By embedding leadership behaviours into KPIs and linking them to business outcomes, the organisation became more agile and future-ready.

Pharma Case Study: Leading Through Transition

Story Context

A leading pharmaceutical company was undergoing a major takeover. The initial anxiety among employees had settled, but the organisation was now in a critical **transition period**. Retaining talent was the top priority, and leaders had to act as **change catalysts** to maintain trust and stability.

The company had strong technical expertise but lacked agility in leadership behaviours. The owner-driven culture was giving way to a more corporate structure, and this shift required leaders to **communicate effectively, make quick decisions, and inspire confidence**.

The Challenge

- **Employee turnover risk:** Attrition had spiked by **12%** during the takeover announcement.
- **Decision-making delays:** Average approval cycle for R&D projects was **18 days**, slowing innovation.
- **Communication gaps:** Employee engagement scores dropped to **68%**, signalling trust issues.
- **Leadership readiness:** Only **40% of managers** were rated as "ready for change" in internal surveys.

Prism Assessment

The company introduced the Prism Framework to assess leadership competencies across 35 managers. Here's a snapshot of three key leaders:

Leader Name	Violet	Indigo	Blue	Green	Yellow	Orange	Red	Refraction Index
Dr Neha (R&D Head)	2	4	1	4	2	2	2	**57%**
Arjun (Operations Head)	2	4	2	2	1	1	3	**54%**
Kavita (HR Head)	3	4	2	2	2	2	2	**61%**

Target Score for all colours: 4.

Interpretation

- **Blue (Communication & Influence)** scored low (avg. = 1.65), critical for managing change and retaining talent.
- **Yellow (Decision-Making)** was weak (avg. = 2.33), slowing project approvals.
- **Orange (People Management)** needed improvement to build trust and engagement.

Sample Questions Used in Assessment

- **Blue (Communication):** *Do you adapt your communication style for different audiences?*
- **Yellow (Decision-Making):** *Do you make decisions based on data rather than assumptions?*
- **Orange (People Management):** *Do you actively mentor team members during transitions?*

Implementation

Based on Prism insights

- **Blue:** Introduced leadership communication workshops and embedded *Employee Engagement Score* into KPIs.
- **Yellow:** Implemented decision-making frameworks and delegated authority for faster approvals.

- **Orange:** Rolled out mentoring programs for high-potential employees to build trust during transition.

HR integrated Prism dashboards into their HRMS, enabling real-time tracking of Refraction Index and linking leadership behaviours to retention metrics.

The Outcome

Within six months:

- Employee engagement scores improved from **68% to 82%**.
- Attrition reduced by **9%**, stabilizing talent during takeover.
- R&D approval cycle time dropped from **18 days to 10 days**, accelerating innovation.
- Leadership culture shifted toward **collaboration and transparency**, reducing resistance to change.

Key Takeaway

The Prism Framework helped the pharma company turn uncertainty into opportunity. By focusing on **communication, decision-making, and people management**, leaders became true change catalysts, ensuring stability and growth during a critical transition.

Automotive Case Study: Breaking Stagnancy Through Leadership Transformation

An automotive company with strong brand recognition and ranked 4th or 5th nationally was facing a puzzling challenge. Sales were growing steadily—up **8% year-on-year**—but profits had remained flat for three years. Dealers were withdrawing, and financial reports showed operational costs were eating into margins.

The company had **25 Regional Managers and 125 Area Sales Managers** in Sales, along with large teams in Operations, R&D, and Marketing. Training budgets were huge — over **₹3 crore annually** — but leadership transformation was missing. At the top, the MD and National Sales Head were asking:

"Why are we spending so much on training without seeing real change?"

The Challenge

- **Sales growth without profit:** Revenue up by **8% YoY**, but profit margins unchanged for 3 years.
- **Dealer withdrawals:** 15% decline in active dealers over 18 months.
- **High training spends:** ₹3 crore annually on leadership programs with no measurable impact.
- **Cultural stagnancy:** Leadership behaviours stuck in operational firefighting mode, not strategic thinking.

Prism Assessment

The company assessed 30 key leaders across Sales, R&D, Operations, and Marketing using the Prism Framework. Here's a snapshot of four critical roles:

Leader Name	Violet	Indigo	Blue	Green	Yellow	Orange	Red	Refraction Index
Abhijeet (Regional Sales Head)	2	3	3	1	1	2	3	**54%**
Divakar (Operations Head)	1	4	1	2	3	1	4	**57%**
Shraddha (R&D Head)	2	4	2	3	1	1	2	**54%**
Kavita (Marketing Head)	1	2	2	4	2	2	2	**53%**

Target Score for all colours: 4

Interpretation

- **Violet (Vision):** Weak strategic thinking → leaders focused on volume, not profitability.
- **Green (Innovation):** Low creativity → no new ideas for cost optimisation or dealer engagement.
- **Blue (Communication):** Poor alignment between marketing and sales.

- **Orange (People Management):** Dependency culture → teams lacked empowerment.
- **Red (Execution):** Operational discipline present but disconnected from strategic goals.

Sample Questions Used in Assessment

- **Violet:** Do you set long-term goals beyond monthly targets?
- **Green:** Do you encourage innovative solutions for dealer retention?
- **Blue:** Do you adapt your communication style for different audiences?
- **Orange:** Do you mentor team members for leadership readiness?
- **Red:** Do you monitor execution against strategic KPIs?

Implementation

Based on Prism insights

- **Sales (Orange):** Introduced coaching programs and embedded *Team Autonomy Score* in KPIs.
- **Operations (Red):** Linked operational KPIs with leadership behaviours through dashboards.
- **R&D (Green):** Launched an "Innovation Sprint" to develop cost-effective product solutions.

- **Marketing (Blue):** Rolled out communication workshops to improve dealer engagement and brand messaging.

HR integrated Prism dashboards into their HRMS, enabling real-time tracking of Refraction Index and linking leadership behaviours to profitability metrics.

The Outcome

Within nine months

- Profit margins improved by **6%**, reversing three years of stagnancy.
- Dealer withdrawals reduced by **10%**, thanks to innovative engagement programs.
- Leadership Refraction Index across 30 managers improved from **54% to 72%**.
- Training costs optimised by **₹80 lakh**, as programs became targeted and data-driven.

Key Takeaway

The Prism Framework helped the automotive company shift from **training-heavy but impact-light** initiatives to a **strategic leadership transformation**. By addressing all seven colours, the organisation aligned leadership behaviours with profitability and growth.

Reflection Questions

- Which case study resonates most with your organisation's challenges?
- What is one takeaway you can apply immediately?
- How will you measure success after implementing Prism insights?

"You've seen the concept, the tools, and the results. Now, it's time to become the change catalyst."

Chapter - 9

Conclusion – Becoming the Change Catalyst

By now, friends, we have reached at the end of this book. So far, patiently, you have gone through this book. I will reiterate my first statement that leadership doesn't happen overnight.

Leadership is not a destination—it's a journey of continuous transformation. Just like a prism refracts light into a vibrant spectrum, a leader refracts knowledge, skills, and attitude into behaviours that inspire growth.

The Prism Framework is more than a tool—it's a mindset. It reminds us that leadership is not about titles or authority; it's about clarity, adaptability, and impact. The question is: **Are you ready to become the prism that changes everything?**

Section A: The Leader as a Transparent Prism

A prism is transparent—it doesn't hide, it transforms. Similarly, leaders must embrace transparency and openness. When you act as a prism:

- You **absorb knowledge** and **reflect clarity**.
- You **bend old habits** and **create new possibilities**.
- You **enable others to shine**, not just yourself.

True leadership is not about being the brightest light in the room—it's about creating a spectrum where everyone contributes to organisational success.

Section B: Continuous Refraction for Organisational Growth

Refraction is not a one-time event. Leadership development must be continuous because business challenges evolve every day.

- Use the **Refraction Index** as your compass for growth.
- Embed leadership behaviours into KPIs, culture, and decision-making.
- Make leadership development a **strategic advantage**, not a checkbox activity.

Organisations that embrace continuous refraction become **leadership-powered companies**—agile, innovative, and resilient.

Reflection Questions: Pause and Think

These are not simple questions—they are meant to challenge your thinking and spark action:

1. **Which leadership colour do you consistently avoid—and why?**

(*Avoiding a competency often reveals a blind spot).*

2. **If your team mirrored your leadership style completely, what would they gain—and what would they lose?**

(*This forces you to see the ripple effect of your behaviours).*

3. **What is one leadership habit you need to "bend" today to create a breakthrough tomorrow?**

(*Refraction starts with bending old patterns).*

4. **How will you measure your leadership impact beyond KPIs—what cultural shifts will prove you've made a difference?**

(*Leadership is more than numbers; it's about influence).*

5. **If you left your organisation tomorrow, what leadership legacy would remain?**

(*This question defines your true contribution).*

Reflection Questions

- Which leadership colour do you consistently avoid—and why?
- If your team mirrored your leadership style completely, what would they gain—and what would they lose?
- What legacy of leadership do you want to leave behind?

Closing Thought

Leadership is light—but only when refracted does it reveal its full spectrum. Be the prism. Transform yourself. Enable others. And create an organisation where leadership is not a role, but a culture.

Appendix

1. Universal Question Sets and Interpretation Guide

How to Use These Universal Question Sets

The following question sets are designed to help you assess leadership competencies using the **Prism Framework**. They can be applied in two ways:

Self-Assessment

Leaders answer these questions honestly to evaluate their own behaviours and capabilities. This helps identify personal development areas.

Prism Assessment (Leader as a Prism)

Leaders assess how they enable these behaviours in their teams. For example, if the competency is *Communication*, the leader should consider: *"Am I creating opportunities for my team to communicate openly and influence decisions?"*

Scoring Guide

Use the behavioural anchors below for every question

- **0** = No capability demonstrated
- **1** = Very low capability

- **2** = Basic capability
- **3** = Moderate capability
- **4** = Strong capability
- **5** = Excellent / Role model capability

Steps to Conduct the Assessment

1. Rate each question on the scale of 0–5.
2. Calculate the **average score** for each colour (competency).
3. Compare the current score with the **target score** (usually 4 or 5).
4. Apply **priority coding:**
   - Gap ≥ 3 → Immediate Attention
   - Gap = 1–2 → Enhance
   - Gap = 0 → Monitor
5. Calculate the **Refraction Index:**

$$\text{Refraction Index} = \frac{\text{Current Score}}{\text{Target Score}} \times 100\%$$

6. Use these insights to create development plans and track progress.

Dual Assessment Templates for VIBGYOR Competencies

Behavioural Anchors for Scoring (0–5 Scale)

- **0:** Never demonstrates the behaviour
- **1:** Rarely demonstrates the behaviour

- **2:** Occasionally demonstrates the behaviour
- **3:** Frequently demonstrates the behaviour
- **4:** Consistently demonstrates the behaviour
- **5:** Role model for the behaviour

Violet – Vision & Strategic Thinking

Why It Matters: Aligns teams with long-term goals and future growth.

Assessment Type	Questions
Self-Assessment	

1. Do you set long-term goals for your department?
2. Do you anticipate market or industry changes and adjust plans?
3. Do you communicate organisational vision to your team?
4. Do you involve stakeholders in shaping strategic priorities? | | **Prism Assessment** |
5. Do you encourage team members to think beyond immediate tasks?
6. Do you provide opportunities for team members to contribute to strategic discussions?
7. Do you mentor team members on aligning their goals with organisational vision? |

Indigo – Integrity & Ethics

Why It Matters: Builds trust and credibility internally and externally.

Assessment Type	Questions
Self-Assessment	

1. Do you consistently enforce compliance policies?
2. Do you challenge decisions that conflict with company values?
3. Do you maintain transparency in decision-making?
4. Do you lead by example in ethical behaviour? | | **Prism Assessment** |
5. Do you create a culture where ethical practices are rewarded?
6. Do you train team members on compliance and integrity?
7. Do you encourage open reporting of unethical practices? |

Blue – Communication & Influence

Why It Matters: Clear communication reduces confusion and empowers decision-making.

Assessment Type	Questions
Self-Assessment	

1. Do you clearly articulate expectations to your team?
2. Do you adapt your communication style for different audiences?
3. Do you provide timely and constructive feedback?
4. Do you influence decisions beyond your direct authority? | | **Prism Assessment** |
5. Do you encourage team members to communicate openly?
6. Do you create platforms for team collaboration?
7. Do you coach team members on persuasive communication? |

Green – Growth & Innovation

Why It Matters: Encourages adaptability and continuous improvement.

Assessment Type	Questions
Self-Assessment	

1. Do you propose new ideas or improvements regularly?
2. Do you allocate resources for innovation?
3. Do you encourage experimentation and learning from failures?
4. Do you implement creative solutions that impact results? | | **Prism Assessment** |
5. Do you create an environment where team members feel safe to share ideas?
6. Do you reward creativity and innovation in your team?
7. Do you mentor team members on problem-solving and innovation? |

Yellow – Decision-Making & Problem Solving

Why It Matters: Quick, informed decisions keep operations smooth.

Assessment Type	Questions
Self-Assessment	

1. Do you make decisions based on data rather than assumptions?
2. Do you involve relevant stakeholders before making critical decisions?
3. Do you resolve conflicts or bottlenecks effectively?
4. Do you evaluate the impact of your decisions post-implementation? | | **Prism Assessment** |
5. Do you train team members on structured decision-making?
6. Do you delegate decision-making authority where appropriate?
7. Do you encourage team members to analyse problems independently? |

Orange – People Management & Coaching

Why It Matters: Reduces dependency and builds future leaders.

Assessment Type	Questions
Self-Assessment	

1. Do you actively mentor or coach team members for career growth?
2. Do you conduct structured performance reviews?
3. Do you recognise and reward team contributions regularly?
4. Do you manage underperformance with clear action plans? | | **Prism Assessment** |
5. Do you provide opportunities for team members to lead projects?
6. Do you encourage team members to make independent decisions?
7. Do you identify and groom high-potential employees for leadership roles? |

Red – Execution & Results Orientation

Why It Matters: Converts plans into measurable outcomes.

Assessment Type	Questions
Self-Assessment	

1. Do you meet deadlines without compromising quality?
2. Do you monitor progress against goals regularly?
3. Do you take corrective action when targets are at risk?
4. Do you prioritise tasks effectively to deliver results? | | **Prism Assessment** |
5. Do you train team members on time management and execution?
6. Do you delegate responsibility for achieving specific KPIs?
7. Do you celebrate team achievements to reinforce accountability?

Interpretation Guide

- **Calculate Average Score**

  Add scores for each question and divide by the number of questions.

- **Apply Priority Coding**
  - Gap ≥ 3 → Immediate Attention
  - Gap = 1–2 → Enhance
  - Gap = 0 → Monitor

- **Track Progress with Refraction Index**

$$\text{Refraction Index} = \frac{\text{Current Score}}{\text{Target Score}} \times 100\%$$

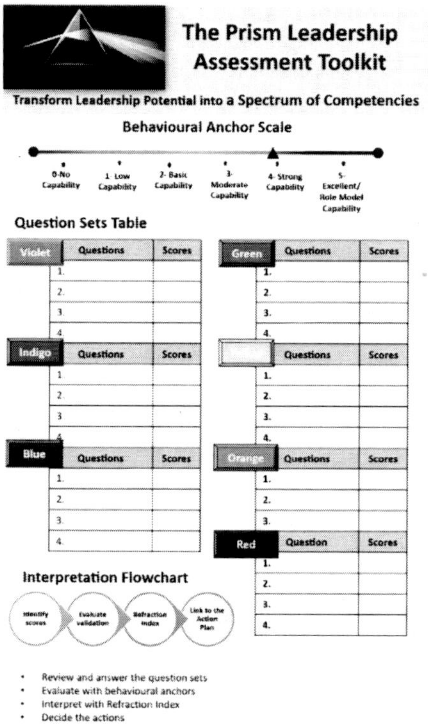

1. Understanding Prism Types and Leadership Complexity

The Prism Framework uses the metaphor of light refraction to explain leadership transformation. Just as prisms bend light differently based on their shape, leaders operate differently based on organisational complexity. Choosing the right prism type helps organisations align leadership development with their structure and goals.

Triangular Prism – Focused Leadership

- **What It Represents**

  A triangular prism symbolises **focused leadership**—ideal for small teams or startups where clarity and speed matter.

- **Refraction Behaviour**

  Light bends sharply into a simple spectrum, representing leaders who prioritise agility and direct decision-making.

- **When to Use**
  - Organisations with limited complexity.
  - Teams requiring quick execution and clear roles.

Square Prism – Structured Leadership

- **What It Represents**

  A square prism represents **balanced leadership**—structured yet adaptable. It suits organisations that need stability and the flexibility to innovate.

- **Refraction Behaviour**

  Light refracts into **multiple, evenly distributed paths**, symbolising leaders who manage diverse priorities—strategy, execution, and people—without losing clarity.

- **When to Use**
  - Mid-sized organisations with multiple functions.
  - Companies transitioning from owner-driven to system-driven culture.
- **Leadership Traits**
  - Transparent decision-making across functions.
  - Balanced focus on innovation, execution, and people development.

Polygonal Prism – Complex Leadership

- **What It Represents**

  A polygonal prism reflects **multi-dimensional leadership**—ideal for global enterprises or matrix organisations.

- **Refraction Behaviour**

  Light refracts into **many angles**, representing leaders who thrive in complexity, ambiguity, and cultural diversity.

- **When to Use**
  - Large organisations with global operations.
  - Businesses managing multiple markets and innovation streams.